Learning Our ABCs: The Adult Version ... Wait! What?

Terri *Lovie* Delaney

There's an *adult* version of our alphabet? Why yes! Yes, there is, because we're all grown up and *A* just isn't for *apple* anymore!

iUniverse books may be ordered through booksellers or by contacting:

iUniverse
1663 Liberty Drive
Bloomington, IN 47403
www.iuniverse.com
844-349-9409

Because of the dynamic nature of the Internet, any web addresses or links contained in this book may have changed since publication and may no longer be valid. The views expressed in this work are solely those of the author and do not necessarily reflect the views of the publisher, and the publisher hereby disclaims any responsibility for them.

Any people depicted in stock imagery provided by Getty Images are models, and such images are being used for illustrative purposes only.
Certain stock imagery © Getty Images.

ISBN: 978-1-6632-2946-5 (sc)
ISBN: 978-1-6632-2947-2 (e)
Library of Congress Control Number: 2021919942

Print information available on the last page.

iUniverse rev. date: 11/11/2021

To our parents, who taught us the alphabet during our wee early ages of life, and to the teachers, then and now, who carry on the tradition. You all deserve an A++ (with a gold star on your shirt collar).

That's right, boys and girls! Or shall I say ladies and gentlemen, you know, because it's more adult-like? My, how the times and world are changing, and with lightning-fast speed to boot. True, life is what we make it, and truer is the fact that life is throwing us curveballs left and right. I personally loved the "good old days," as I'm sure many of you did as well. Life seemed easier. Hell, life *was* easier. And today, with all the chaos, craziness, and commotion every minute of every day, we need to find a little piece of peace while taking deep breaths and eating (*insert favorite food choice here*); mine is chocolate. No, it's cheese. No, it's—shit. No, not *that* shit! I simply just can't make a simple decision these days.

To cut a long story short, join me, guys and gals, and together let's learn the grown-up version of our A-to-Z alphabet! I hope your takeaway will guide you to a calmer, cooler, and more collected state of being. Come on. We all know we need this. You'll see.

OK, let's go! Let's do this!

A is for *appreciate*. What I appreciate most are the little things, especially the ones that don't cost a thing: a hug, a smile, or a quick "just dropped in to say hello" message.

What do you appreciate?`

B is for *beautiful*. The most beautiful things in the world are the things I feel in my heart and see with my eyes. Oh wait. How could I forget? My nose and the aroma of baking cookies, BBQing, the ocean, a puppy's breath, a bonfire—all so deliciously beautiful!

What is beautiful to you?

C is for *celebrate.* We have the chance, in any given moment on any given day, to celebrate everything that is good like love, sunshine, chocolate, and laughter.

What do you like to celebrate?

D is for *dream*. All of us dream while sleeping at night. We all also dream about accomplishing something, visiting somewhere, and winning the lottery. I know I do!

What dreams do you have?

E is for *embrace*. To embrace yourself, your value, your knowledge, and your importance is to accept all of you–the good, the bad, and yes, sometimes the ugly. Give yourself a great big hug!

What do you embrace?

F is for *fabulous*. When I think of fabulous, I think of someone or something that makes me feel—well, fabulous! Fabulous as in happy, content, and special. Feeling fabulous makes others feel the same.

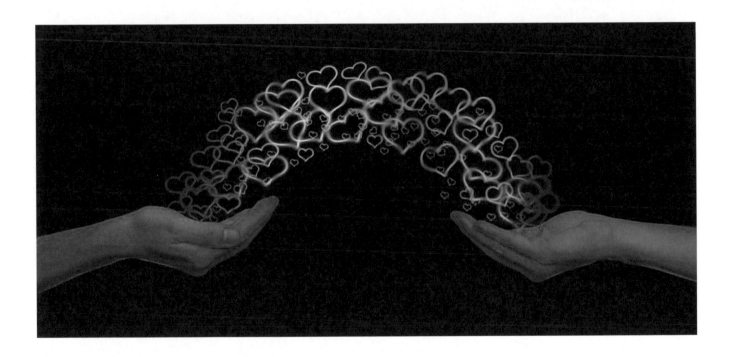

What is fabulous to you?

G is for *grateful*. Be grateful for the truth in good things, good people, good times, and most importantly of all, the good in ourselves.

What are you grateful for?

H is for *happy*. Be happy *now*–not when something goes right and not while wishing something great may happen soon. Be happy *now*!

What are you happy about?

I is for *inspiration*. I find inspiration from so many people, many whom I've never even met, yet they share their inspiration with the world in a book, a blog, a movie, a look, a picture, and so forth. Inspiration is everywhere!

What does inspiration do for you?

J is for *joy*. Joy to the world! Joy to you and me! I also love the joy in the eyes of someone who just found out great news, hearing a baby's giggle, and having frozen chocolate bites in my freezer!

What brings you joy?

K is for *kindness*. How hard is it to share kindness? Look for the kindness that is given to you, and look to see how easy it is to share your kindness with someone else. It's kind of cool and the kind thing to do!

What does kindness do for you?

L is for *live, love, laugh.* I couldn't choose among the three Ls because we can all *live* our best lives, *love* each other (as well as ourselves), and *laugh* until our bellies hurt! They're all of the best things we can do. Combine them all together and you'll always win the jackpot! Best recipe and no calories!

What do the three Ls mean to you?

M is for *meaningful*. Meaningful moments are my favorite moments! There are so many people, places, and things that are meaningful and all around you. Just look. They're there!

What is meaningful to you?

N is for *nice*. It's nice to be important, but it's so very much more important to be nice.

What is nice for you?

O is for *outstanding.* Whatever you are doing in your life, no matter what it is, give yourself credit and love because that's what makes you outstanding.

What is outstanding to you?

P is for *patience*. When one more nasty word, one more dirty look or one more flippant attitude strikes, have patience my dear. Breathe deep for patience, indeed, is a virtue beyond compare.

What is patience to you?

Q is for *quiet*. Ahhh, quiet. It's one of the best things we all need and deserve. No wonder peace and quiet go together and make a great couple.

What does quiet do for you?

***R* is for *respect*.** It's easier and most polite to respect everyone in the same way you want to be respected. If you give it, you'll get it.

What is respect to you?

S is for *sassy*. I love the word *sassy* because when I feel sassy, I feel happy, sparkly, and lighthearted. Special mention: there was once a fantastic friendship (that I still hold close to my heart) whereby I was the "Sassy" to her "Cheeky" because we shared happy, sparkly, and many lighthearted moments together!

What is sassy to you?

_T_ is for _trust_. Whatever you do, trust yourself, your gut, your head, and your heart. It's hard sometimes to trust others, and it hurts when we realize we can't. So before anyone else, _trust yourself_!

What is trust to you?

U* is for *unique. We are all wonderfully unique. No one else in the world will be or can be as special and extraordinary as you are.

What is unique to you?

_V_ is for _value._ Value the people, places, and things in your life. To value is to treasure and cherish because they and you are worth it. And that is incredibly and wonderfully priceless!

What do you value?

W is for *wishing*. Wishing upon a star, wishing you were at the beach, and wishing for spaghetti and meatballs with baked garlic-cheese bread dipped in olive oil (that didn't add pounds onto you) all have significance and meaning. Therefore, keep your wishing going, going, and going on some more. (And now I'm hungry! 😊)

What are you wishing for?

X is for *XOXO*. Because you can never give or get enough hugs and kisses.

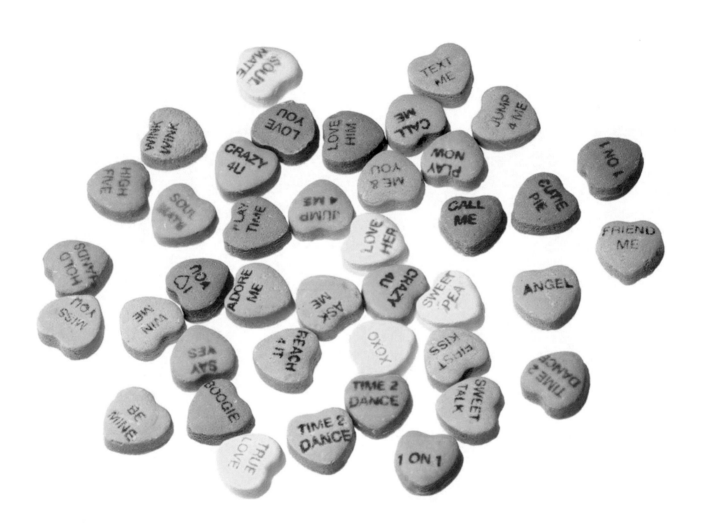

What is XOXO to you?

Y is for yes. I used to say no a lot in the past. I'm learning to say yes more often. When the people, places, and things line up together with a happy, hopeful outcome, I will then give them a yes!

What is yes for you?

Z is for *zest*. We all want to have zest in our lives, don't we? I sure hope we do because zest contributes to our enjoyment, delights, happiness, gladness, contentment, bliss, and comfort, to name but a few. Zest is the best!

What brings zest to you?

Printed in the United States
by Baker & Taylor Publisher Services